Incipient Poetic Thoughts..

Anitesh Pattanayak

INDIA • UK • USA

Copyright © Anitesh Pattanayak, 2021

All rights reserved. No part of this publication may be reproduced, stored in a retrieval system, or transmitted in any form or by any means, electronic, mechanical, recording or otherwise, without the prior written permission of the author. Any resemblance to actual people, living or dead, or to businesses, companies, events, institutions, or locales is completely coincidental.

Paperback ISBN: 978-1-954399-58-7

eBook ISBN: 978-1-954399-59-4

First Published on 2nd March 2021

Published by Walnut Publication
(an imprint of Vyusta Ventures LLP)

www.walnutpublication.com

USA

6834 Cantrell Road #2096, Little Rock, AR 72207

India

#722, Esplanade One, Rasulgarh, Bhubaneswar – 751010

#55 S/F, Panchkuian Marg, Connaught Place, New Delhi - 110001

UK

International House, 12 Constance Street, London E16 2DQ

When Anitesh was a dear colleague and during several years of close interactions, I realized about another side of his personality and with a different dimension. But we were drowned in work pressures and I could see that side only in his professional writing and presentations.

After reading his beautifully articulated Memorabilia in his maiden book 'Shades of Camaraderie' back in 2019, I could connect with his flair and what I felt about his other side many years ago.

Anitesh has shown that one who is in the space of emotional connect with several personalities, sees the world in a different way and through the eyes of others. As in the introduction in the poem 'Along the Warmth of Time', one could visualize the poetic mind and creative spirit. A poet's heart connects with his conscience and sees beauty in every fragment of nature while expressing his feelings in a beautiful rhythm.

I am delighted that Anitesh, with his divine gift, is now embarking on his second publication 'Incipient Poetic Thoughts'. I am sure that the poems in the book will be received by the readers with great affection acknowledging the effort, dedication and imaginative instincts.

My best wishes to Anitesh on this joyful occasion and also for the continued creativity in the future.

K. Ravindranath
Ex Senior Vice President and Whole-Time Director
L&T Hydrocarbon Engineering Ltd.

"

Though I always knew 'Anitesh' as a good conservationist, never for once I knew that he had such a passion for poetry. It was therefore a bit of a surprise when I read few of his poems from the overall collection that he is to publish in March'2021.

While prose writing is fairly simple, poetry requires inspiration, a flight of imagination and a good grasp of the language. "Anitesh' has displayed all these in his first publication and am very confident that we can definitely look forward to more of his literary works in course of time.

As he plans to launch his first book on his parents 54th Wedding Anniversary, I would like to wish his parents good health and togetherness for the years ahead and take this opportunity to wish Anitesh many more literary laurels in the years to come.

K Shanker
Ex-whole time Director
Technip India

"

I am extremely pleased to see that Anitesh is publishing his collection of poems "Incipient Poetic Thoughts". In the recent years of our friendship, Anitesh has always shown his creative side in English literature. He is a sensitive soul and one feels the depth of his feelings in his works. The delicate and subtle treatment of the subject and the fluid expressions make very pleasurable reading. He is a keen observer, and a deep awareness of the surroundings are expressed in his works. The writer has positioned himself at the center and his outpouring of feelings can be seen and felt. I liked the beautiful and magical composition of words. I have read some of his poems and they have touched my heart. I am sure we will see many more such work from Anitesh in future. I wish him all the best in his literary journey.

Dipti Ranjan Nanda
President
Malaysia Odia Community

"

It is a delight to read the poems from the volume *Incipient Poetic Thoughts*. A floral scent wafts through the interiors of the reader's heart as the verses are read. The lines have a lyrical grace and suppleness to evoke the contours of the delicate feelings of longings and losses. The poetic persona's landscape changing with seasons is overlaid with a broad swath of moods ranging from melancholy to nostalgia to contentment. The lyrical voice seldom gives way to mawkish sentimentalism or fanciful exuberance. Rather, it shows self-restraint in good measure, which is most suitable for the ageing persona in the twilight hours of life. Reading through the verses one clearly sees a path through the mushy undergrowth of worldly experiences leading towards a clearing on which falls gentle sunshine streaming through the verdant foliage, as it were. One would do well not to give any name to this supremely enlivened moment, for good poetry never defines any experience or pins it down to a formulated phrase. It is as T.S. Eliot said in his *Four Quartets*: "a raid on the inarticulate".

I sincerely hope the poems will warm the cockles of the reader's heart.

Ashok K Mohapatra, PhD
Fulbright alumnus (Columbia, Yale)
Professor of English
Sambalpur University, Odisha, India

"

My association with Anitesh began two-decades ago, as colleagues & friends, which continues till date. For me, Anitesh is an institution and a thorough professional with passion and aspiration like his icon Roger Federer. He has a strategic & decisive mind with keen eye for investment ... be it money, time or relationships. In spite of such qualities, he is extremely humane & people's man.

On the personal side, Anitesh is a great sportsman, has flair for writing, has very good sense of humour and loves natural 'beauties' .... I cherish my association with this man. Personally, a huge value addition.

Anitesh is responsible son, doting husband and adoring father. My write up will be incomplete if I do not mention about his beautiful wife **Ipsita** ... fantastic cook and a great host. She has played a vital role in shaping Anitesh and the family. The manifestation is visible in their well-groomed and well-educated children ... **Adarsh and Anisha.** My wife and I are extremely happy to have Anitesh and family in our lives.

Back in 2019, we missed to attend the function of release of his earlier book – 'Shades of Camaraderie' due to professional commitments. My wife & I take this opportunity to **CONGRATULATE** his parents on their 54th marriage anniversary & wish **'ALL THE BEST'** for successful publishing of his second book – 'Incipient poetic thoughts' ...

GOD Bless !!!

Mrs. & Mr. SD Navare
Executive Vice President
L&T Hydrocarbon Engineering Ltd.

"

Some of the poems composed by Anitesh on romantic and philosophical themes are quite interesting to read. Apart from work, I always admire Anitesh as a person who follows his passion such as sports and literature and we discuss about it from time to time. I had the opportunity earlier in 2018, to meet his large family in Bhubaneswar, Odisha, during the launch of his book 'Shades of Camaraderie', when I became aware that literature/ arts/ journalism runs in the family. I wish him best of luck for the success in his endeavor to publish the compilation of his poems and emergence as a poet par excellence. I am confident that readers will enjoy the poems. I also look forward to more such literary work by Anitesh in times to come.

SR Balvalli
Senior Vice President
Technip India Limited

K. C. Patnaik
MBA (USA), M. Inst. PM (UK), AMIMA, FIMM
Member NIPM, Past President of Rotary Club

CENTRAL CHINMAYA MISSION TRUST
SANDEEPANY SADHANALAYA
Saki Vihar Road, Powai Park Drive,
MUMBAI - 400 072 INDIA.
Tel.: (91-22) 28035157/28034970

E-mail: kcpatnaik@chinmayamission.com
Office: ccmtpublications@chinmayamission.com
Mobile: 9819404969 / 9172784455

Life is a series of experiences from womb to tomb by constant contacts with the world outside with multiple objects and nature. Everybody feels; but few really analyze, understand and educate from such experiences!

The garland of poems in "Incipient Poetic Thoughts" by Shri Anitesh Pattanayak is a reflection of feelings, deeply studied, sincerely analyzed and appropriately expressed in words for the readers to reflect on them to understand the world in various aspects in a realistic manner.

I congratulate Shri Pattanayak for having been able to compile his sensible thoughts appropriately, while being engaged as a professional engineer.

I genuinely hope that these poems would provide food for thought to all; particularly those readers who ardently seek to study their experiences from world outside.

(K.C.Patnaik)
General Manager
Books & Publications

"

This is both a testimony and an ode to someone who I have known for 12 years. He is a free thinker, and an incipient poet who touches you profoundly with the simplicity of his thoughts and words. His poems are tranquil and contemplative. Less formal, less ceremonious, and better suited to quiet reading. They are a true reflection of who he is as a person – Calm, composed and poised.

As a reader, his words reach out to us as the experiences narrated are relevant, reflective and recent. Anitesh maintains a fine balance and steers clear of both unnecessary inflections as well as a dry, flat reading.

What Anitesh has also taught me is that it is never too late to allow that "Light Within" to emanate. There is nothing you cannot achieve if you put your mind to it, irrespective of where you are in life. I am extremely glad that he has crossed over that bridge and is coming out with " Incipient poetic thoughts ".

I am sure, the book will make a mark in the minds of all its readers.

Let the Light Within shine brighter each day!

Good Luck!

Divya Raj
Asst. General Manager
L&T Hydrocarbon Engineering

"

I am overwhelmed to read and cherish such beautiful words, written in form of poems, which came out of your creations. Your writing style is very natural and your words appeal the heart more than eyes and ears. I would like to wish you a great amount of good wishes and best of luck for the future and we appreciate your business with us and thank you for giving us a chance to serve you.

Uttam Agarwal,
Chief Business Officer,
La Premier,
Bajaj Capital Ltd.

Incipient Poetic Thoughts...

Author's Note:

Following the promise during the publication of my first book titled *'Shades of Camaraderie'* in Mar'2019 (limited distribution), this is my second book, a compilation of few of my poetic thoughts, a mix of dreamy, colorful and abstract poems. The hypothetical ideas and themes sometimes emerged from nowhere or while in different states of mind and sometimes while interacting with the external world. The motivation to write perhaps comes from the love of writing and the legacy of the family and it is such an effective option to communicate and express. I am still an amateur writer, but the hobby of writing is gradually becoming a consistent practice. Moreover, I have realized over last few years that discovering the passion of writing in various platforms is like a vitamin and has immensely helped me in my professional and personal fields with increased enthusiasm, energy and efficiency.

The year 2021 continues to be impacted by COVID19 and its new variants and we are finding ways and means to live with it, in spite of the launch of vaccine administration programs across the globe. Regardless of all kinds of disruptions, our mother Earth is in some respite with record reduction in GHG emissions reduction. Perhaps it is a good time to explore incipient literature by new writers as a leisurely activity and therefore I hope, you will enjoy the poems that I have managed to present to you. Your valuable feedback and assessment would encourage writers like me to widen the skill of writing in the coming years. I may not stand tall, I may not catch the castle, but I can still shine.

'The mother is weightier than the earth; The father is higher than the heaven'. I take this opportunity to dedicate this book to my parents (Prasanna Chandra Pattanayak and Shaila Patnaik), who are celebrating their 54th marriage anniversary on 2nd March'2021. As per their wish, the earnings from the sale of this book will be donated to an under-privileged girl child of their choice. Also, my wife Ipsita and me are happy that the release the book coincides with our 25th marriage anniversary, which we celebrated in February'2021.

I request that if possible, and in order to enjoy the poems better, please get a paper (hard) copy instead of the e-book and read during your leisure time. Also, please buy the book as a gift for your near and dear ones to extend the circle of happiness of reading.

"Note: The themes of the poems are imaginary and any resemblance what so ever is purely coincidental"

Thank you and look forward to your feedback.

Anitesh Pattanayak
16D, Budheswari Engineers Colony
Bhubaneswar, Odisha, India
Email: anitesh.pattanayak@yahoo.com

About the author

Anitesh Pattanayak is an engineering professional with around three decades of industry experience in the energy sector in India, Middle East and Asia Pacific regions. Currently, he is working in Kuala Lumpur as a 'Business Development Director'.

'*Incipient poetic thoughts*' is the second book being published by the author. He published his first book titled '*Shades of camaraderie*' in March'2019, capturing his interactions and experience with fifty people from both personal and professional spheres.

He also writes articles on verities of current topics, which are published in various magazines and websites.

Contents

Section-1 1

('Love is an act of endless forgiveness')

    1.   Back in my younger days 3

    2.   Never dared to say 5

    3.   Return of the enigma 9

    4.   Your visit to the town 12

    5.   The world could be ours tonight 15

    6.   Do not insist 18

    7.   I am so glad 20

    8.   Iconic night 22

Section-2 25

('Success is simply a matter of luck. Ask any failure')

    9.   Along the warmth of time 27

    10.   I was speechless 30

    11.   Time will say 33

    12.   Sister! Get richly blessed 36

    13.   Friends for ever 38

    14.   Chasing the dreams 40

    15.   Oh Traveler 45

16.	I didn't care enough	47
17.	Same world but another frame	50
18.	When the night gets deep	52
19.	The World can be one	54
20.	My inner soul	57
21.	I'll return to pursue	61

Section-3 65

('You can't blame gravity for falling in love')

22.	Through the years	67
23.	Scotch and Ice	69
24.	The tree in the courtyard	71
25.	Destiny beyond hope	73
26.	You are no more mine	76
27.	The search continues	79
28.	I am restless tonight	82
29.	Whom are you after	84
30.	Days without you	86
31.	It wasn't a dream	88

Section-4 91

('Change is the law of Universe')

    32. Mohan to Mahatma 93

    33. Running down a dream 96

    34. City of Kuala Lumpur 98

    35. Down the track 101

    36. Arise Oh traveler 103

    37. Under the bridge 105

    38. Let's get back home 108

    39. Hour of solitude 110

    40. Pleasure and amusement 112

    41. Oh Skyscraper 114

    42. May be, may be not 117

Section-1:

('Love is an act of endless forgiveness')

Anitesh Pattanayak

1. Back in my younger days

I recall the Spring, back in my younger days
The warming weather, the wandering clouds
The growing trees and the blooming flowers
But most of all, it was You
Your soaking in the Sunlight
and the dancing in the daffodils
You brought attention to the drowsy flowers
and the magic coat of clover on the planes
We walked deep in the woods, breaking the rules
We knew Spring would come again
Long ago, back in my younger days

I recall the Summer, back in my younger days
The Blazing Sun, the heated earth
The buzzing bees, and the dusty hot wind
But most of all, it was You
Summer's kiss on your lustrous skin
Filling your veins with summery light
Your freshness in the afternoon pool
The thrill of the ice cream and the watermelon
Making the days longer and the nights shorter
We planted the garden believing in tomorrow
We knew Summer would come again
Long ago, back in my younger days

I recall the Autumn, back in my younger days
The shading yellow leaves, the skeletal deciduous trees
The dancing wind, and the busy moving squirrels
But most of all, it was You
You made the air fragrant, crisp and free
Gusting through each swaying tree
Touching your face to bring up the smile
Stealing the sultry summer heat
Precluding the woes of winter
You and me and our innocent age
We knew Autumn would come again
Long ago, back in my younger days

I recall the Winter, back in my younger days
Escaping birds, the chilling wind
Biting temperature, and the languishing Sun
But most of all, it was You
The tree branches bending down
To touch your delicate fingers
Choir of birds singing with you
breaking the loneliness
You sparkled when the snow fell like glitters
The barren lands enlarged our imagination
We knew Winter would come again
Long ago, back in my younger days

2. Never dared to say

First glimpse was special, even if you didn't notice
The stature, the attire and the emergence
The square glasses and the radio voice
A whacking introduction of a flying career
And I knew 'An angel has arrived'

You didn't take time to galvanize
To become a darling and synchronize
The exuberant smile, the effort-less elegance
Stimulating interactions and the distinguishing appearance
But I never dared to say, 'You influenced me'

I went crazy at every opportunity to meet you
To get closer and prevail better than the rest
To smell the aroma of the cologne around you
To see the textures of the curved lips and the shining hair
But I never dared to say, 'You captivated me'

Dancing waves acknowledged the drowning Sun
The red sky and the chirps of the birds
We embraced the evening
And persisted through the night
The waves became quite
And the morning began to bright
You wanted to go home
And I never dared to say, 'You fascinated me'

Season of love arrived, but opportunities missed
You left for a long assignment, just when I was to solicit
The unbearable pain of separation
And the feelings and its reverberation
I had no choice but to wait till you return
We spoke many times
But I never dared to say, 'You uneased me'

Your message about the return
Gave me goosebumps
I cancelled my leave
Although you didn't confirm the date
The excitement of the reappearance
Of the ageless Angel
But I never dared to say, 'You rejuvenated me'

However long the night, the dawn always breaks
Not only you returned
But sanctified my impetuous passion
I had to redefine the boundary of my happiness
The limit of my youthfulness
But I never dared to say, 'You ratified me'

The phone calls, the coffees,
The long-drives and the twilight dinners
The love we generated,
The memories we accumulated
The deepest feelings we shared,
The emerging bond we established

You became the most beloved
And me the most precious
But I never dared to say, 'You enlarged my dreams'

Your exponential upraise at work was conspicuous
The skill-set, the enviable attitude and your leadership
The skyward ambition and the spirited determination
We parted as you moved on to pursue the destiny
The night was stressful
But I never dared to say, "You unsettled me"

As you live in a clover and rolling in it
And I started to turn over a new leaf
I will always be proud of the little chance that you gave
That led my steps aboard
On the grass of richness and fulfillment
To smell your sweet presence
And become your ardent fan
The sun and stars
Can never hide you from my eye
But I never dare to say, "You continue to mesmerize"

"You and me and our innocent age"

3. Return of the enigma

The day was winding and the evening was setting in
The pouring shower was washing the roads anew
I occupied the corner table near the window
The thrilling sensation and inflated anticipation
At the return of the imperishable angel, the ultimate winner

The cloud started to clear, the rain started to recede
The music started to play, the lights began to shine
The mind stated to race, the butterflies started to multiply
As the time of your coming was drawing nigh

You arrived, you emerged, you hypnotized
You looked almighty beautiful
The skin as smooth, the cheeks as rosy
The eyes star filled, the smile as breathtaking
The voice as harmonious, the fragrance as refreshing

Seeing you in flesh and blood, I gasped for breath
Your touch chilled me, I turned to a statue
The glow was luminous, I lost my virtue
All my preparation flied out of the window
The memory that slept so long awaked from below

We settled down as I regathered myself
The wine tasted sweet, the music became melodious
The phones went silent and the candles began to glow
It was all about your overwhelming journey and its influence
As we walked down the road to reach the sea shore
the waves of renewed romance appeared in galore

The night at the sea was an ultimate pleasure
Your eyes an enigma full of captivating treasure
We danced like the butterflies fragile and soft
Following your aroma, all inhibitions were lost
Hearts met again like the waves resting upon the seashore
As we lay there, silently gazing at stars above
Experiencing the undying passion and the lost love

Thought of your departure at the advent of the light
My heart bled tear as we hugged tight for the night
The fact that the sand castle will break again soon
My mind yearned for the youthful poetic tune
The possibility that the waves will again take you far
My soul got disoriented amidst the wonderment of air
You looked weary as you left the coast
I wanted to make up for the years lost
The evening rain and the candlelight dinner
the accompanying waves and the twinkling stars
Influence of your youthfulness and the unfolded night…
It was time to return to the realm of the light

I returned to the shore the next day and again
Every time, there was a new dawn grazing the ocean
In anticipation of the golds of your eyes
Echoing the shadows of your words
Encouraging me to hope
Arrival is really a departure
And which we call departure, is only a return

4. Your visit to the town

News of your visiting the town
Spreading the fragrance far and wide
Morning, Evening and Night
Water, land and air
The soul and the rest
Imagination and its lost boundaries

Dreams have never been so sweet
Thinking the whole night
And then in the morning and again
Mind and the heart, filled with thoughts
Such an indulgent state

You are an enlightment
Your presence, your smile
Your voice and your touch
And everything else that you do
Such a privilege

The road that you travel
The space that you occupy
The place that you rest
And the people that you meet
You just blossom everywhere
Such an inspiration

Every time I praised
You smiled, you acknowledged
Every time a barrier was found
You knew how to transform
Love everywhere, every moment
Such skillful artistry

The journey of love
The difference between living and dying
Going through these years
Carrying each of these imaginations
Privileges, experiences and inspirations

The news of your visiting the town
Spreading the fragrance far and wide
Thousands of wishes filling the breath
Every wish is better than the rest
It doesn't matter
Such an overwhelming condition

Oh pretty woman! Have mercy
Don't remove the curtain from your face
For I may lose the bearing of my existence
And that I may not endure the pain
The pain of living beyond your departure…

"It was time to return to the realm of the light"

5. The world could be ours tonight

If you see
the most beautiful girl in the town
Tell her, here I am..
And that I want to hold her again,
in the middle of this desert tonight,
to feel her freshness,
that fills the silent air
and to believe in the falling star
She and the beating of her heart
It's such a beautiful night
Tell her that I'm waiting
and that the world
could again be ours tonight

If you see
the most beautiful girl in the town
Tell her, here I am..
And that I want to climb with her again
to the top of the mountain tonight
The time-less peaks
and the down land planes
The inspiring nature's sights
and the fairy echoes
She and her sweet little nod
It's such a beautiful night

Tell her that I'm waiting
and that the world
could again be ours tonight

If you see
the most beautiful girl in the town
Tell her, here I am..
And that I want to be besides her again
In the wilderness of this wood tonight
To feel the softness of her steps
To believe in the music of the jungle
She and the silkiness of her hair
It's such a beautiful night
Tell her that I'm waiting,
and that the world
could again be ours tonight

If you see
the most beautiful girl in the town
Tell her, here I am..
And that I want to be wet again
As the clouds shed the tears of joy
and Each flower, branch and tree
telling me to believe
in the beauty of the rain
and in the song of my happiness
She and her heart-felt hug
It's such a beautiful night
Tell her that I'm waiting

and that the world
could again be ours tonight

If you see
the most beautiful girl in the town
Tell her, here I am..
And that I want to ride the bike again
In this full-moon night
away from the city light
on the lonely narrow causeway
alongside the swollen river
illuminating shadows of the past
The warmth and safety
of her stretched arms
She and her animated youthfulness
It's such a beautiful night
Tell her that I'm waiting
and that the world
could again be ours tonight

6. Do not insist

It's late in the evening
The moon is shining bright
The breeze is blowing light
Your make-up looks sublime
Your heart is sounding upbeat
and everything else seems just right
Keep holding my hand
else, I will be lost
As the night gets deeper
As the moon goes higher
Just agree to my request and
tonight, don't insist to withdraw…

I feel the magic because I see
the love in your eyes
and because
you don't realize how much I love you
My life gets to its edge
when you begin to rise and go,
Oh my beloved!
As the passion flows
as the romance conquers
Just agree to my request and
tonight, don't insist to quit…

Incipient Poetic Thoughts...

The innocence of the cool weather
that defines the beauty and love tonight
and makes me feel so nice
Who knows what will happen tomorrow
Let me be in your arms tonight
Just agree to my request and
tonight, don't insist to retire

Life is all about limited time
but these moments are timeless
Let us not lose this time, my beloved
Let's not have a life of regret
Let the flame burn
Let this memory be stamped for ever
Just agree to my request and
tonight, don't insist to bid adieu…

"To believe in the falling star"

7. I am so glad

Every now and then
Time and time again
I've felt crushed
I've felt such isolated
wondering why and where
Just about the time
when I think I can't hold on
You're always there for me
Don't know if a man loves a woman
or if a boy likes a girl
But I know how much I needed you

Every day, I join the bandwagon
Trying to make my living,
Some days up
and then falling down the ladder
Still trying to stay afloat
Just when I felt
nothing could get any better
I realized,
I still love you more than ever

Today as I watch the Sun
setting down on the horizon
and the birds flying around

returning back to settle down
I know I'm entangled in the polluted air
Don't know the direction
Don't know the destiny
But beyond everything, on the other end
I know, you may be there
With your softest hand
and the kindest heart
still loving me as before
I'm so glad that it's still not the end...

8. Iconic night

Hug me, embrace me
This is such a cool evening
Pale crescent moon shining
like a silvery claw in the sky
The blanket of stars stretching to infinity
And the silence of your presence..
It's a rare occurrence

Hold me tonight
Such nights may not come again
We may not experience this unification
Your warmth and fragrance
filling the air around me
The state of ultimate bliss
may not be a reality anymore

These moments are special
We are destined to merge
Let me look at your eyes
as much as I wish
Not sure when again
there will be another chance
So come closer to me
sit alongside me
and love me

Let this night stay for ever
The sun will set
The moon will raise
The stars will blink
The rivers will flow
The waves will dance
But you may not return
Your eyes may not shower such love again
Let me hear your inflated heartbeat
Let me enjoy the silence of the fusion
Embrace me
for this beautiful evening may not come again

"Blanket of stars stretching to infinity"

Incipient Poetic Thoughts...

Section-2

('Success is simply a matter of luck. Ask any failure')

Anitesh Pattanayak

9. Along the warmth of time

Today it feels like a mixed dream
I listen to the quiet breeze
I see the blue sky
and the green leaves
and TIME has gone by
and perhaps TIME to amend

As I look out of my Balcony
I see the apparent redness
of the sunrise
I see the chirping birds on the sky
I notice the buildup
The usual rush, the usual noise
and I try to realize
what I gathered and what I left
what I gave and what I acquired
and TIME has gone by
and perhaps TIME to amend

I still search for YOU in the crowd
in the empty fields
and in the soaring clouds
In city lights and passing cars
On the winding roads
and in the wishing stars

I wonder today
Where you would be
and TIME has gone by
and perhaps TIME to amend

Today is a beautiful day
It's a special day
I move my hand
through the clean air
I think of our accords
and the denials
Our coming together
and falling apart
The hits and the misses
that brings the history
and the warmth
that reverberates
and TIME has gone by
and perhaps TIME to amend

Today, as all these
and much more
unite with the soul
Oh King of time since its dawn!
I don't need a fortune or fame
but I need
a stroke of serendipity
a bit of coincidence

I will live as long as it takes
for the best is yet to come
Many rivers to cross
many mountains to discover
They may say
what they want to say
But I just feel alright
to go all the way

10. I was speechless

Meeting you the other day
to discover the endless pain
the vast anguish
the underlying fear
and the consequent fright
I was speechless

Your obvious silence
and the justified stiffness
even after so much of crisis
so much of agonizing treatment
and your eagerness
to bounce back
I was speechless

I just went back
in the time line
Your smiling face
and the enthusiasm
The hospitality
and the culinary expertise
For I remember
the joys that we once shared
You showed in so many ways
how much you cared

Present emerged
and I was speechless

I noticed the change
in your appearance, it had to..
But the core in you
and the expression in the eyes
were unchanged
I did not know how to act
how to behave
I couldn't find words
to speak or anything to share
I was speechless

I am not sure
if each of us
have a predefined destiny
If in the darkened valley
there's still room to pray
But I tend to believe
that you will find that one star
to guide your ship
That you will find the Panacea
to remain safe from further grief
and that you can win
the eventual battle
I left you
I was speechless

Anitesh Pattanayak

"You will find that one star to guide your ship"

11. Time will say

News channels, newspapers,
You tube and the social websites
Haven't they changed
The way we and our children see
the past, the present and the future
Redefining the democracy
the constitution
the geography
and the fundamental rights
Blunder or Success
Emptiness or Inclusiveness
Non-violence or belligerence
Not we but Time will say

Perhaps a short-term detour
from the core of fundamentals
and the human rights
to remove the status quo
of history and the consequences
Perhaps for the benefit
in time to come for the stakeholders
Will it be sooner than later
Not we but Time will say

Perhaps there is
a robust and inclusive plan
beyond the rhetoric
Taking along
the local collaborators
and their support
Will the terrorism vanish
and the killings stop
Will the education bloom
and the industry proliferate
Will the children play
and the movies be shot
and will the tourists flow
Not we but Time will say

Perhaps the measured aggressiveness
will not escalate further
No war, no nukes,
No loss of life
For only they know
what it means to be living in the bunkers
and taking the incoming bullets
and what it is like
to land on the other side of the border
Awarding Param Vir Chakras
posthumously
is no consolation
for spent lives do not return
Not we but Time will say

Perhaps the religions
and the faiths
will regroup and flourish
For after all it is all about
righteousness, forgiveness
compassion and love
Hope the banks of the Jhelum
and the Dal Lakes will refuel life
Neither Leftists nor the Rightists
neither green nor the saffron
Let only the Indian-ness
spread all around
Not we but Time will say

There is always a 'my view',
a 'your view'
and a 'real view'
We spend our life
fighting for my view
But, in the meantime,
What is the destiny
what is the real view
Not we but Time will say

12. Sister! Get richly blessed

A daughter, A friend
a wife, a mother
a colleague, a teacher

But for me
You are a dear sister
who makes me feel special
irrespective of whatever…
Those silly fights and stupid mischiefs
The joys and the sorrows
that we shared once under one roof

As years pass by
You will be a treasure
Always there in a countless ways
Your shoulder to lean on
Your lap to rest on
Sharing your spice-filled experience
tolerating my satires and sarcasms

We may not be always together
but we always travel together
on Life's journey
The special trust and love
that only we can find

Incipient Poetic Thoughts...

Today get indulged...
Cut cakes
eat more
treat friends
get richly blessed

"Those silly fights and stupid mischiefs"

13. Friends for ever

Friendship is like a shining light
always cheerful and bright
It is a treasure of time
Wealth of countless and spicy experience

It takes away the loneliness
Encouraging to share the happiness
Friends see dreams together
To be filled sometime sooner than later

Those silly fights and stupid mischiefs
the joys and the sorrows
that the friends share together

From schools to the universities
Friendship teaches how to face life's complexities
Friends hold hands when needed the most
Midas touch and the troubles are lost

The friendship evolves for ever
The strength of the bond grows stronger
The journey and the road may diverge
The bond and the support always converge

Friends meet to depart
but only to meet again..

Incipient Poetic Thoughts...

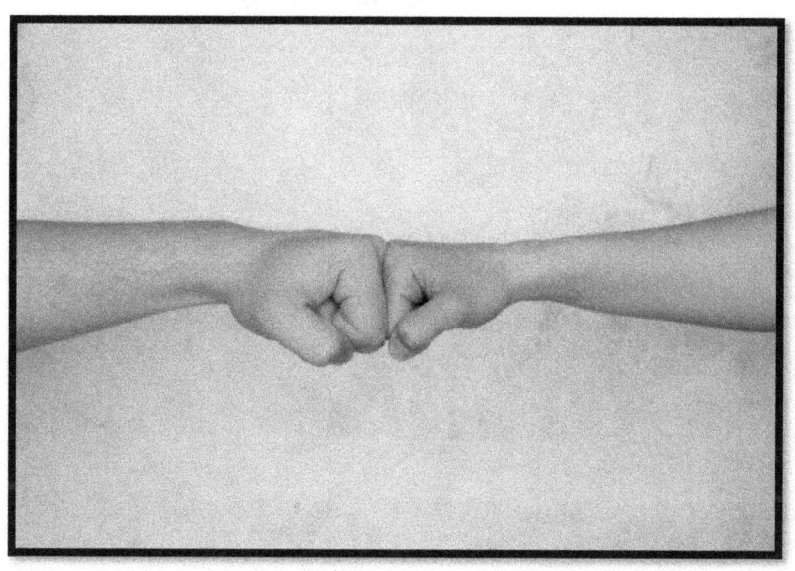

"Friends see dreams together"

14. Chasing the dreams

Chase your dream
Fearlessly, limitlessly
Stand a little taller
Run an extra mile
Grind yourself
Fall, fail and raise
Catch the castle
Shine but do not stop

Smith and Virat
Best than the rest
One aims to be the best player
and the other as the king
Every time they fall, they bounce higher
making it difficult to track the records
Chasing the dreams

Teen-aged Greta Thunberg
Traveling from Europe to America
on an emission-free yacht
raising awareness
on human-induced global warming
Taking charge for a cooler earth
Chasing the dream

Dreams come in the night
for few perhaps in the day
in various sizes, mostly colorless
invariably unclear, rather incomplete
hard to grasp, difficult to remember
Complete those dreams
fill those colors
Dare to live your fairytale

Banerjee and Duflo
Fighting global poverty
improving human conditions
Grass-root micro-economic models
Nobel Prize further fuels
the mission of unfinished hunt
Chasing the dream

K Sivan,
the modest ISRO man
and his farfetched fantasy
To land on the Moon
Inevitable failures
Dire consequences
Stubborn perseverance
Chasing the dream

There is always another mountain
one more uphill battle
It isn't about how quick you get there
it's not about what's on the other side
it's the climb

Long-legged Sindhu
Even after failing repeatedly
demonstrated tenacity
to become the first Indian
as the world champion
Today, she sees herself in the mirror
and says, 'I haven't yet found the greatest'
Chasing the dream

Young Jamyang Namgyal
The fresh parliamentarian
His pursuit to convert new Ladakh
to prominence and modernity
Despite severe resistance
from within and across the border
Showing the courage found within
Chasing the dream

Dreams can be unreal
Fights can be lost
Faiths can be broken
Wins can be rare
but you made the choice

Having come this far
you can't turn back
Just as the flowing rivers
So, get up and get going

Chase your dream
Fearlessly, limitlessly
Stand a little taller
Run an extra mile
Grind yourself
Fall, fail and raise
Catch the castle
Shine but do not stop

"Complete those dreams, fill those colors"

15. Oh Traveler

Oh traveler,
Do not stop, do not fear
Keep trying, keep exploring
Miracles are no contradictions to nature
Eventually you will reach the destination
Somewhere, far away, in this world

Your mind is flowing free
It's trying to find the shore
Wandering with too many ideas
Deliver when life demands highest effort
Your wishes will come true
Eventually you will reach the destination
Somewhere, far away, in this world

Your egos are interrupting you
Fill in your heart with gratitude and joy
Angels fly because they keep themselves light
Irrespective of the circumstances,
Show your enthusiasm and don't be tight
Eventually you will reach the destination
Somewhere, far away, in this world

The King of times takes care of all
Whenever the cloud of hard time gets dark
He brings light, he shows the way
giving you the opportunity to learn
Eventually you will reach the destination
Somewhere, far away, in this world

Oh traveler,
Do not stop, do not fear
Eventually you will reach the destination
Somewhere, far away, in this world

16. I didn't care enough

I know you won't return
like the daily sunrise
But I feel your warmth
every day, every moment
But I didn't care enough
about the moments
that we were together

I was overwhelmed
every time by your presence
You brought me smile
you showed me care
you taught me wisdom
but I didn't care enough
about the moments
that we were together

Your vibrating voice
the unending energy
all-encompassing camaraderie
I feel everywhere
In my house, in my car
in my heart, in my ear
But I didn't care enough
about the moments
That we were together

I will say everything
about you, for ever
until no one is left to hear
and then, it will not matter

What matters
in this interim life is
that You shared
some of your
short-lived time
with Me

I know you won't return
But I will maintain
the radiant lamp
that you lighted
till I depart
this unkind, violent
and rather
complicated mankind

Incipient Poetic Thoughts...

"I know you won't return"

17. Same world but another frame

It is such a gorgeous sunrise
brightening slowly across the sky
It has been the same all these years
the same moon and the same stars
the same old land and the same mountains
It's the same world, but another frame

As the days go by
My fate and the fortune
seem to fade away
A bit entangled in life's purple past
Working on the dreams I planned to try
Wondering what the future still holds
It's the same world, but another frame

Such a vicious cycle
Young ones grown old
Little stars are growing young
setting higher benchmarks
Technology has held us spellbound
Skyscrapers, automation, 5G and beyond
EV cars and the sophisticated drones
Greenhouse gases and its consequences
It's the same world, but another frame

It's been so long
Friends have changed
Family members have spread far
Colleagues have grown ahead
Kids have their points of views
Fellow travelers have chosen different paths
Society that I knew is dismantled
It's the same world, but another frame

Every evening
When the Sun goes down
Sailing down behind the Sun
The heart gets a bit numb
trying to restore the soul again
wishing to travel far, to find a house
and to be free from
the hatredness
the fear of others' ascendance,
The greed of capitalistic attachments,
and from going after the false stars
It's the same world, but another frame

18. When the night gets deep

When the night gets deep
dreams come on display
entranced by illusions
in all its colors and grandness
caressed by gentle breezes
spreading its network
leaving the thoughts of despair
showing the world of good

And then the morning arrives
replacing the best of the night
and the decorated nest
crushing them as if none mattered
leaving the clouds of reality
bringing life back to the mortality
believing that the dreams will live on

Always wanted to forget
the memories that long faded away
the mountains that couldn't be ascended
the flights that couldn't be boarded
the disputes that couldn't be resolved
It keeps coming back in sleep
as if it is present and real
Even if dreams on display aren't true
but a feeling that the dreams will live on

It's all about hiding everything
The endless seas and the dark woods
The missed dawns and the luminous dusks
Moving again with the fortune
To find a new destiny, a new horizon
To build fresh dreams of fulfillment
To believe in the unpredictability of life
and again, saying hello to sleep
and the night gets deep again

19. The World can be one

Visualize there's no boundaries
No rich, no poor, no religion
No military spending of trillions of dollars
No environmental worries, no pandemics
Humanity on a different pursuit, a new quest
It isn't difficult perhaps
Nothing to eliminate or be decimated for
Each creature on this earth
living life in perfect harmony
perfect balance, perfectly synchronized

It may be a dream
But nothing irrational to believe
That someday all will join the dream
Just as the rivers meeting the sea
to unite, to merge
the world can be one

Not very long ago
Our very own Mahatma advocated
The world has enough for everyone's needs
but not everyone's greed

Visualize we give up acquisitiveness
Surrender every so often

few things that we don't need
to those who are not as lucky
It isn't difficult perhaps
Many of us wonder as we turn older
Can we adopt comradeship
allowing every soul to share the world
not only today but for long

It may be a dream
But nothing unreasonable to believe
that someday all will join the dream
Just as the stars in the sky
twinkling together
sharing the space
in perfect harmony
The world can be one

Visualize there's no heaven up
and no hell below
Only the sky, the space,
and the beautiful and healthy mother earth
It isn't difficult perhaps

Alongside joy,
lives the potential for even more joy
Alongside our united hearts,
lives the potential for stronger unity
And alongside our surrender,
lives the potential for more tolerance

It may be a dream
But nothing illogical to believe
that someday all will join the dream
just as the colors of a rainbow
staying together
forming the extraordinary arc
in perfect congruence
The world can be one

"The same Moon and the same Stars"

20. My inner soul

Voice coming from within
like the transparent rain
falling from the sky
dancing, twisting and turning
across the vast landscapes
without differentiating
experiencing happiness and suffering
filling through my empty wit
embracing me, speaking to me

Our creation, the duration,
our trials, tribulations,
illnesses and the calamities…

Oh Sakshi,
The witness consciousness!
The inner guiding light!
that I bow and lay down
Guide me, untangle me
Enlighten me…

Broken images, incomplete pictures
appearing from everywhere
across the cosmos
seemingly restless

like fish in an aquarium
blustering aimlessly
from the bottom of the seabed
to the farthest of the stars
as they make their ways
across the visible universe
capturing my imagination

The mother, the father,
the friend and the companion,
the knowledge and the wealth…

Oh Sakshi,
The witness consciousness!
The inner guiding light!
that I bow and lay down
Guide me, untangle me
Enlighten me…

State of happiness, shades of despair
limitless, boundaryless
shining like a million suns
filling through my mind
reaching every creature
every epitome, every atom
across the habitats

It can never be cut into pieces by any weapon,
nor can it be burned by fire,
nor moistened by water,
nor withered by the wind..

Oh Sakshi,
The witness consciousness!
The inner guiding light!
that I bow and lay down
Guide me, untangle me
Enlighten me…

Our hands made strong
by the Architect of mankind
How long shall we spread the hatred
Let's move forward in triumph
singing the new song of freedom
across the mountains, across the oceans
across humanity and beyond

Well-being, peace,
Progress, fulfillment, auspiciousness
Equality and balance..

Oh Sakshi,
The witness consciousness!
The inner guiding light!
that I bow and lay down
Guide me, untangle me
Enlighten me…

"The inner guiding light"

21. I'll return to pursue

You held my hand
as I was absorbing the wisdom
of your Buddhism and the awakened Buddha
Buddham saranam gacchami
Dhammam saranam gacchami
advocating Thought, Speech, Action,
Effort, and Mindfulness…
Weeks of my insightful practice
It seems no different from the rest
just as the water in the ocean
Peace for everyone, for me and you
I will to return to pursue…

You stood by me
As I was grasping the knowledge
of your Christianity and the sacred bible
Preaching, Adoration
Petition and Thanks-giving
You say humans are images of God
and Jesus ensures salvation of humans…
Weeks of my astute application
It seems no different from the rest
just as the air in the atmosphere
Peace for everyone, for me and You
I will return to pursue…

Your kindness towards me
As I was experiencing the depth
of your Hinduism and the Upanishads
The Dhams and uncountable Gods
Tat Tvam Asi - That Thou Art
Transforming ignorance to knowledge
Impure to pure to liberation…
Weeks of my awakening engagement
It seems no different from the rest
just as the raining water from the sky
Peace for everyone, for me and You
I will return to pursue…

Your patience to allow me time
as I was decluttering my tangles
about your Islam and the sacred Quran
La ilaha illa Allah
Wa-Muhammad rasul Allah
Urging to believe, pray, fast and donate
and making everyone more human…
Weeks of my committed exercise
It seems no different from the rest
just as the color of the leaves
Peace for everyone, for me and You
I will return to pursue…

Your humble welcome
as I was exploring the secrets
of your Jainism and Vardhamana Mahavira

The Tirthankaras, Arihants and Jinas
recommending Non-violence,
Renunciation, Tattvas and Vratas
Universal love, Equality and Respect...
Weeks of my rewarding sessions
It seems no different from the rest
just as the dancing waves in the sea
Peace for everyone, for me and You
I will return to pursue...

Your illuminated support
as I was following the rituals
of your Sikhism and the Guru Granth Sahib
Guru Nanak to Guru Gobind Singh
The incomprehensible Waheguru
Teaching Truth, Equality,
Prosperity and Conduct...
Weeks of my enlightening cognizance
It is no different from the rest
just as the twinkling stars
Peace for everyone, for me and You
I will return to pursue...

Section-3

('You can't blame gravity for falling in love')

22. Through the years

Through the years
when you look at me
seeing things that others can't
All my fears and apprehensions
failures and worries
You get into my soul
and read me like nobody can

Through the years
You believed and trusted
and come what may
whether or not we agree
during certainty or uncertainty
we learned to find a way

Through the years
even when I am wrong
You let me go through it
and that has helped me
making me discover and rediscover
again and again

Through the years
and when my dreams fall apart
when they can't be reassembled

I turn around and you are there
shining in your eyes
smiling at me, believing in me
kissing my tears away

Through the years
when I spoke unilaterally
You let me speak
acknowledging me
empathizing with me
allowing me to realize
that I am not always right
helping to explore other alternatives
and never letting me down

Through the years
You turned my life around
helping to find the sweetest days
Our grown up children
beginning to understand
our unspoken and undemonstrated love
As long as it is ok
I'll stay right here with you
for more experiences
loving you through the years…

23. Scotch and Ice

Scotch and ice in the glass
You say I am high
And I say, it's such a special state
as if there is no gravity
You say, I am blustering
but I say, I am freeing myself

Scotch and ice in the glass
You say, I am unstable
but I see the sunshine of your eyes
You say, I am flattering
and I say, this is just the beginning

Scotch and ice in the glass
You say, I am in no control
and I say, there is no boundary
You say, I may fall down
but I say, I can fly with you
higher than the kite and the eagle

Scotch and ice in the glass
You say, go to sleep
and I want to stay awake
You say, rest when the dawn arrives
but who wants this night to get over

It's time to discover
For morning may not arrive

Scotch and ice in the glass
You say, be careful
and I say, whatever will be, will be
You just hold on to me
for I'm not leaving you now
You say, time to go home
and I say, let the destiny unfold tonight
let the future be ours to see
Whatever it is worth
It's no more relevant anymore..

"I want to stay awake"

24. The tree in the courtyard

That day, many years ago
The tree in the courtyard
was filled with flowers
The air was filled with the fragrance

You plugged one of them
and put it on your thick hair
as you entered my home
full of dreams and color
your overwhelming presence
as if everything else did not exist

As the twilight arrived
The full-moon appeared
from behind the clouds
under that perfume-filled tree
A mix of darkness and the light
playing hide and seek
and the dreams started to unfold

The rainy night that followed
We walked out on the lonely road
and then the ride on the bike
Your holding on to me
whether for the safety or spontaneous
didn't matter as I felt the warmth

The benefit of not being seen
The safety of secrecy and indulgence
The feeling of wetness and the moisture
The two rivers uniting at the confluence
Becoming one stream and flowing further
Remaining merged for ever

The clouds disappeared in the morning
The dream of merger vanished
Such a difficult reality
No more flowers
No rides, no holding hands
It was just another day as usual

The tree in the courtyard
still standing tall
Flowers continue to blossom
but the fragrance is missing
no more hide and seek

Yet I recollect the face
The flower and the perfume
The shining eyes
and the softest of touches
anticipating the impossible
as the years pass by…

25. Destiny beyond hope

It was a long drive to your town
in that stormy and irresistible night
The sound of thunders
the rain and the strong breeze
giving me courage

Your message after so many years
to meet at your address
Unaware of your current status
Looking at the message again and again
The lotus eyes and the rest
that I looked last, many years ago
Once again reappearing in the mind
as if it was yesterday

The closer I got to your town
more restless I became
apprehension of the unexpected
pinching myself repeatedly
to ensure it wasn't another dream

So many thoughts in the mind
about you filling my soul
as the rainstorm continued during the night
What if the narrow wooden bridge breaks

The only way to enter your town
What if the car engine fails

The night was still deep
The bridge was intact
The car was fine
It wasn't difficult to find the address
The electricity was cut off
as the rain continued to pour
I knocked at your door
again and again
even if I saw the hanging lock
I replied to your message
several times and again

The hurricane passed
The rain stopped
The street lights glowed
The day broke, the dawn arrived
The behemoth lock on your door
as if asking me to give up
But the hope whispered to persist
and I waited..

The delusion ended
Days, months and years passed
No more messages from you
and yet the prayer of faith continues
for there may be a destiny beyond the hope

Incipient Poetic Thoughts...

the dreams started to unfold

26. You are no more mine

The first sight long ago
The lotus eyes, the silky hair,
the slimness and the simplicity
The eyes met and we smiled
and I thought you were mine..

Every time you appeared
You looked special
You blossomed
Your lovable heart
like a bottomless transparent lake
and I could see
my image at every layer
You acknowledged
and I thought you were mine

You called me
Our first coffee together
Your blinking eyes
The radiation of your skin
The vibration of your companionship
We exchanged our identities
The promise to meet again
and I thought you were mine

Our supper in the evening
at a place of your choice
the menu of your liking
the light to suit your brightness
The incomparable florescence
the incomplete stories
sometimes logical
and often crazy and unreasonable
and I thought you were mine

Your invitation to your cozy house
The overwhelming beauty
The silence of the music
The sweetness of the fragrance
The irresistible temptation
The freedom and the bliss
and I thought you were mine

Your departure
The warmest hug
The tears in the eyes
The dreams about the future
The world of imagination
My devotion and offerings of love
Detachment of soul from the body
and I thought you were mine

Passing of time and its shadows
Your success and growth
like a timeless star
no illusion, no falsity
just as the holy river
flowing tirelessly
to find the ultimate reality
and even today
I resist to believe
You are no more mine…

27. The search continues

Saw her the first time
in a sunny afternoon
at the tea-stall
outside the office
She looked exhausted
sun-burn was visible on her skin
She spoke to me ever so softly
as I was looking at her
A special attraction
behind the tired eyes

She perhaps needed a friend
someone she can trust
a man who can understand
what she was going through
I never wanted to know
if that was me

It became a ritual
Same time, same place, every day
weeks after weeks,
months after months
She told her stories tirelessly
and I listened to each of them diligently
discovering her and the unspoken beauty
every single day..

And then, as they say
everything in life changes
I waited from the afternoon till the evening
and the next day, next week…
Waiting in anticipation
became the new ritual

I traced to her hostel
but she was gone
I met her acquaintances
but no success
I reached her town
but her parents had no clue

I went from one place to another
towns, hostels, shops,
temples and hotels
End-less journey of suspense
in every direction
The land, the water and the space
ignoring all the rumors
looking at so many faces
hoping to rediscover
the magnetic face
So many untold stories
Undiscovered beauty
Broken dreams and disappointment

Every night when the sun goes down
The moon appears and the music plays
and I lie on the bed
thinking about what she said
Oh sweet-girl, it's not fair
You belong to this night
You belong to me..

"I thought you were mine"

28. I am restless tonight

Please appear, Oh epitome of love!
even if only for a moment
Tonight, my mind seems disoriented
My heart seems empty,
Whatever form you are in
whether real or illusion, physical or tangible
Show your radiance, let me get a glimpse
My soul will get peace
Don't make an excuse
Tonight, I am restless without you

Please emerge, Oh everlasting eternity
Let your shadow of glory fall on me
In the middle of reality and fantasy
In between my belief and illusion
I have nothing to do with the name, shape and color
Let just the pleasure of uniting with you
be the filling moment tonight
Either ecstasy or misery
either enlightment or ignorance
I don't have any second wish or prayer
Be merciful
Tonight, I am restless without you

Please emanate, Oh Angel
In this world of delusion
Let the love entangle us
Deep meditation, ultimate engagement
Let your blessings overwhelm my devotion
The night and the shining moon
The incessant stories of this glorious moment
Let tonight be our night, a fulfilling dream
The ultimate truth, supreme treasure of life
Tonight, I am restless without you

"The dreams started to unfold"

29. Whom are you after

Oh my subtle heart!
Whom are you feeling for tonight
Why are you looking so happy
Who has shadowed you
How true and how much illusion

Why is tonight filled with such music
Such sleepy state, yet can't close the eyes
Why is the mind occupied tonight
Someone special amplifying the hope
and conquering the thought and the mind
Oh my subtle heart!
Tell me whom are you after
in this wakeful night

The restlessness and the inflated heartbeat
It's difficult to rest tonight
Rolling from one side to the other
Seems to have found some one
Has she arrived at the courtyard
Will I get a glimpse tonight
and will the endless wait get over
Oh my subtle heart!
Tell me whom are you after
in this sleepless night

The air is filled with moistness
The night seems so rosy
The sky and the stars
looking at me tonight
recognizing the moment
and hinting at her arrival
I can hear the song
and see her lotus eyes
Oh my subtle heart!
Tell me whom are you after
in this jittery night

"I am restless without you"

30. Days without you

The days with you
As special
as the days without you
The anxiety, the concern
The endless waiting
and the hope
Every moment
very special and intimate

And then as the day passes
and the night arrives
The restlessness, the sleeplessness
and the anticipation
of seeing you the next day
The overfull mind and soul
engrossed with such thought

Your transcending
Form of appearance or disappearance
Whether you come or not
My eyes and heart get filled
Whether with you or without you
Makes no difference to me
Like a glowing star in the night sky
Always present

irrespective of cloud and rain
It doesn't matter

The days that you do not come
Gives time to rewind
The memories of our togetherness
From the moment of your appearance
Till your departure
The smile, the coffee
The stories, the silence
The pleasure, the pain
The overflowing love
and the infinite state of uniting

Days after days
Weeks after weeks
Your choices and decisions
To come or not to come
Perception of fulfillment or
The state of vacuum
Bliss of your presence or
Realization of your absence
The consequence is immortal
With or without you…

31. It wasn't a dream

I dream of the stormy sea, the falling stars
I dream of broken castles and erupting volcano
But finding you in my arms wasn't a dream
The sublime eyes, the honeyed voice
The consistent aroma
The comfort of your cloths
right next to me
throughout the night
It wasn't a dream

I dream of rainbow and its colors
I dream of the overflowing river and its noise
But listening to your heartbeat wasn't a dream
Your never-ending stories
Your controlled smile
When I complemented
You asked not to stop
right next to me
throughout the night
It's wasn't a dream

I dream of the field of sunflower
I dream of the power of the green mountain
But holding your hand wasn't a dream
The softness of your hand

Incipient Poetic Thoughts...

The silkiness of the hair
The irresistible color of your lips
right next to me
throughout the night
It wasn't a dream

I dream of a kingdom and the pleasure
I dream of the space and the galaxy
But loving you in the middle of the night
wasn't a dream
The calmness of overflowing enchantress
Your transcending state of bliss
right next to me
throughout the night
It wasn't a dream

"Whether with or without you"

Section-4

('Change is the law of Universe')

32. Mohan to Mahatma

Bless us Oh Bapu
Mohan to Mahatma
Simplicity at its powerful best
Vaishnava Jana Tu tene kahiye
Je pida parayi jane re....

We want to see you here
We want to be with you
You and your philosophy
Liberation from violence
Adhering to truthfulness
Removal of oppression
Race, class, gender, religion and beliefs
Relevant then, today and tomorrow
Timeless and eternal

Superficial celebrations
Empty rhetoric about you
No more good for us
It's time to reappear
Re-establish and revalidate
Your religious, social and political ideologies
Beyond South Africa and India

You left us in a hurry
Too much burden of independence
and to carry on with the vision
We and our leaders
seem to be directionless
politically, socially and religiously
Reading prepared speeches
Spreading hatredness
Selling your dreams
To achieve the miserly desires
Polarized mankind, amplified hatredness
Imbalanced earth and the lost harmony
One step forward, two steps back

Bless us Oh Bapu
Mohan to Mahatma
You must get recarnated
As a political activist, social reformer
Religious thinker and as a writer
Resuming your train journey
Reinstating 'Vasudhaiba Kutumbakam'
Satyagrahas and message of non-violence
'Hind Swaraj'
The gospel of love and self-sacrifice
You must do it all over again

You will face greater resistance
socially and politically
Bullets may pierce your chest again

But your inspiration, vision and work
could remove the ignorance
The Sun of truth could shine on earth
and our miseries may dissolve
Therefore, we want to see you here
We want to be with you

Bless us Oh Bapu
Mohan to Mahatma
Simplicity at its powerful best
Raghupati Raghav Raja Ram
Patita Pavan Sitaram
Ishwar Allah Tero Nam,
Sabako Sanmati De Bhagawan…

Bapu! It's time for your return…

"Timeless and eternal"

33. Running down a dream

I'm running down a dream
Going wherever it leads
Miles and miles away
Across the seas
Beyond the setting Sun
Into the oblivion

Even if the feet is paining
Some money in the pocket
A head full of dreams
With wide possibilities
In all colors and extravaganza
The magic and the splendor
Unfolding one after another
As I'm running down a dream

Moving with speed of light
Without any fear or might
Looked like a King's treasure
Prolonging the happiness forever
The wind is breathing low
The stars are signing bright
The waves are making noise
And the rain continues to pour
As I'm running down a dream

The dream castle in the air
The paradise of eternal bliss
Skies of azure and fields of green
Music of love and wind of change
Me and my destiny in the dream
I see, I feel, I experience
And then I lose the theme
And the process begins again
As I'm running down a dream

The mind begins to work
Running from pillar to post
One predicament to another
From dilemmas to the plights
In shaping dreams to reality
Mind is searching for an app
Looking for a machine
That can make things easier
Converting visuals to 'brick and mortar'
Accuracy doesn't matter
As long as I live in the heartfelt dream

34. City of Kuala Lumpur

The city of Kuala Lumpur
The greenery and the mountains
The parks and lush gardens
Varied cultures, histories and modernization
Petronas tower, Batu caves
Putrajaya and Little India Brickfields
A popular global tourists destination

The city of Kuala Lumpur
No discrimination of humanity
The Malayas, the Tamils
the Chinese and the rest of the nationalities
Practicing respective beliefs fearlessly
Celebrating Hari Raya, Gong Xi Fa Cai and Deepavali
Living in true harmony and seamless synchronization
and offering so many public holidays
bringing cheers and smiles

The city of Kuala Lumpur
The climate and its adequacy
People say it is either dry or wet seasons
But I find the dryness and wetness everyday
keeping the temperature and humidity in control
However sometimes, the air gets affected
by the incoming haze from across the border

The city of Kuala Lumpur
Offering verities of cuisines from around Asia
to suit the taste buds of the people
The famous Nasi Goreng and Nasi Lemak
Options of Thai, Indian and Indonesian menus
and the local Mama restaurants
displaying colorful and fresh food all-round the day

The city of Kuala Lumpur
and the Bahasa Malaysia
With several loanwords
from Sanskrit, Greek and Latin
Aksara, Angur, Bahasa, Bahaya
Bakti, Bhumi, Dirgayu, Kursi and Manusya
are only few among many

The city of Kuala Lumpur
Even if only a few years
But one feels as if living for many years
and wishing to stay for even more
Langkawi, Penang, Terengganu and Pahang
and yet many more places to explore
It is such a privilege

Anitesh Pattanayak

"Bringing cheers and smiles"

35. Down the track

Many years ago
Came a young boy and a girl on a track
walking many miles with loads on their back
They put down the bags
where they thought was the best
Built a cottage on a no-man's-land
built their work and a cozy store
cultivated the land besides the lake shore

Soon came many travelers down the track
They never walked beyond
They never returned back
Then came the houses, the schools, the hospitals…
The professionals, and then the rules
The buses, trains and the trucks with more loads
Soon the dirty old track was a noisy road

Further came the industries, and the technologies
And then the hard times, the fights and the wars
Radio spoke about the confused state
The noisy track was in a disarray
like an overflowing wild river losing its balance
as if everything going to freeze tonight

Instead of work, everything was shut down
there's no cozy store, no ploughing, no more loads of trucks
People have to pay for their misses and the faults
They have to harvest fresh again
The birds up on the wires and the road side poles
seem to fly away from this old track
singing out their music
all the way down the road

The boy and the girl
could soon forget the sufferings, but not those nights
when life was on a race between win and loss
They wanted to run away just as those birds
out of this darkness and into the light
Instead of wild overflowing rivers,
to the distant virgin mountains
From the anger on the streets,
to the unexplored camaraderie
From complex red lights on the lane,
to the greenery of new pastures

But all these signs saying,
"sorry, but we're closed"
All the way down the noisy track....

36. Arise Oh traveler

Arise Oh traveler, its already dawn
The Sun is in display
It's time to move on
So many travelers on the road already
Why are you still sleeping
Even if you feel tired
You have to advance
Long journey to the unknown
You have to negotiate alone
The house, the courtyard
It's all nothing when you are gone
Don't you know
You are here only for the night
It is not your house
Even if you stayed here for the night
Every traveler who comes here
leaves after the night
Where from and where to
this place is only temporary
The early you realize
the better you will be prepared
for the journey ahead
Some travelers have already left
Others are following you
No one can hold on to this place

The travelers you assume as companions
You will never find them on the passage
The relationship is only temporary
All of them will disappear sooner or later
All of these only for a night
Such is the illusion,
Far from the ultimate reality
Therefore Oh traveler!
Get up and get going….

"All the way down the road"

37. Under the bridge

I looked at her
At a crossing under the over-bridge
in a hot afternoon
She seemed ill-fed but busy
with her naked children
at a corner under the bridge
The ragged saree wrapped around her
the uncombed hair and the hardened skin
Yet a smile on the face
as she shared a bread
with the muddy street dog

I found her again another day
cooking on a temporary fire
The torn saree
insufficient to cover her body
Washing the broken utensils
with the waste-water from the street
sweeping the dust to clean the place
for the begging children to return and rest

I followed her again
under the evening street light
and the impact of headlights
of the vehicles passing by

She was speaking to her children
They were still naked
I was curious about their conversation
Perhaps sharing her experience
for a creating a better tomorrow

I saw her again
on the way back home from the Airport
It was past mid night and cold
She was lying in open with the babies besides her
Covering them with a cloth
Ensuring their safety and well-being
The rejected saree still around her
The street dog sleeping cozily next to her
The tired eyes and the ears
Seem to be unaffected
by the brightness of street light
and the sound of the overloaded trucks

Next time I was crossing the bridge
She seemingly disappeared
Neither her, nor the little naked children
I looked at the dirty street dog
It looked confused
missing the hospitality
Perhaps trying to find a new friend

Hopefully, she would be fine
somewhere in a different territory
Perhaps someone could replace
the torn saree with a new one
and some oil and a comb
to straighten their tangled hair
New dresses for the children
Fresh vegetables and a warm blanket
A home and some love...

38. Let's get back home

It seems a good time
to get back home
breaking the endless voyage
along with the irreversibility of time
The body seems to be weary
The feet is getting slower
The mind is jumbled up

Sooner than later
The rumbling may stop
The rainwater may subside
The force of the wind could diminish
The cocoons will release the golden butterflies
and the rainbow will sprinkle blessings

So, let's get back home
to the safety of mother's warmth
and under Father's watchfulness
and the princely pampering of grandparents
Let's be a child once again

Rediscovering the innocence
The fun and the friends
Playing on the empty and littered streets
Cutting the kites to taste victory

Incipient Poetic Thoughts...

Tired and hungry
Such childish nuisances
Rewinding the foggy memories
And dreaming again…

"Let's be a child once again"

39. Hour of solitude

It's a windy morning
The decorated temple
and the occasional sound of the bell
echoing to far distance
spreading the blessings of the Lord
The little lamp about to extinguish
The empty approach road
The Pandit riding the cycle back
to his next destination
My closed eyes and the unanswered prayer
It's return to the hour of solitude

It's a sunny afternoon
The solitary house and the chimney
Black smoke polluting the clean air
The barren abandoned courtyard
The lonely flower enjoying the breeze
The dirty street dog resting under the shed
The hummingbird looking for nectar
My hope is beginning to raise
It's return to the hours of solitude

It is a windy evening
The hill, the blue sky and the colorful rainbow
Synchronizing with the twilight

The valley and its landscape
waiting for the fall of the night
The birds settling down
The noise is getting silent
My dreams starting to take shape
It's return to the hours of solitude

It is a windy night
The clock is touching midnight
One moment, the moon behind the cloud
and then, the cloud behind the moon
displaying lunar synthesis
The street lamp muttering in the dark
The noise of light drizzle and the rough sea
The blue spark of the lighted match
My memories throwing up high and dry
It's return to the hours of solitude

"Its return to the hours of solitude"

40. Pleasure and amusement

Pleasure and amusement
Here it comes
and vanishes next moment
ever so fluctuating
It seems as a reality
and then it reappears as an illusion
just as a mirage on the vast desert
The more one gets nearer
it goes farther away

Tireless effort to acquire more
to aim more, to fight for more
to be determined
to eliminate all barriers on the way
After all, it's about fulfilling the desire
but losing the way more often
Miscalculations and lost attempts
The complexity and the mental agony
Bouncing back and attempting again

The bliss of possession
No one is spared
It attracts one and all
Irresistible, inevitable
Such is the anticipated pleasure

even if it is only momentary
The instant a possession is complete
the desire manifests to the next
A step up, an increased appetite
Redefining success
Leading by example

The golden deer in the jungle
It invites, it drags
projecting a castle
As one attempts
it disappears and reappears
smiling, ridiculing
continuing to attract
and then abandoning at nowhere
The cycle of veiling and projecting

No more urge
No more delusion
No more falling prey to the golden deer
Remaining within the boundary
Removing the ignorance
Realizing the error of veil and projection
Attempting to find
the ultimate pleasure
of discovering the light within

41. Oh Skyscraper

The beautiful woodlet
at the far end of the town
The eyes get filled
with the beauty of the greenness
Diversity of plants, mangroves and flowers
The sun finds it difficult to penetrate
The sounds of the swinging trees
as the wind blows through the orchard
in the summer afternoon

You the magnificent tree
offering beautiful flowers and tasty fruits
and much more…
without considering anything your own
You offer no resistance what so ever
It's always about serving others
displaying every time
compassion and pleasure of giving
The beauty and the aroma of your offerings
touches the mind and the soul
Consuming them, selling them, exporting them
making medicines and furnitures
enjoying the profit and success
You get nothing, you expect nothing

Incipient Poetic Thoughts...

All kinds of birds
ordinary and extraordinary
in various colors and sizes
taking shelter in you
experiencing the flavor of your fruits
Verities of animals and insects
do not spare you either
Your infinite limit of tolerance
years after years
generations after generations

You wither the severity of the nature
and the impact of changing seasons
the heat, the cold, the storms and the floods
in spite of the pain and the ferocity
You stand and deliver tirelessly
Just as mentioned in Bhagwat Geeta
'Karmenyabadhikaraste ma phalesu kadachana..'

Will you teach Oh skyscraper!
the art and spirit of your exhibition
spreading the shades of happiness
never giving up..
Every time, I am at a crossroad
I come to you
and watch you and your manifestation
You always offered a place
allowing me to realize and discover
as if you say 'stay a little longer, take it little easy'

You have always filled my heart
with light and shine
You provide the answers
albeit I'm unable to practice

"Muloto Bramharupaya,
Madhhyetu Bishnurupeni
Agratah Sivarupaya,
Bruhkyarajaya te namah"

"The sounds of the swinging trees"

42. May be, may be not

Oh King of time!
I don't know who you are
What is your form and shape
Where you exist
What are your boundaries
What you do
Are you the only truth
The ultimate witness
May be, may be not

But, when I see the sky
The celestial dome on which
float the Sun, Moon, planets, and the stars
and the illusion of its blueness
and yet much remains to be known
That I start to assume
You may be somewhere there
Could you be that unknown
May be, may be not

When I see the Sun
and it's infinite energy
like billions of tons of dynamite
every second, for millions of years
and yet much remains to be known

That I start to enquire
Are you as or more powerful
Are you that unknown
May be, may be not

When I watch the stars in the dark
Billions of luminous balls of gas
Hydrogen and Helium
and the incomprehensible galaxy
and yet much remains to be known
That I begin to research
Are you somewhere beyond it
Are you that unknown
May be, may be not

When I see the Ocean
and it's far reaching vastness
controlling Earth's weather
Home to millions of plants and animals
and yet much remains to be known
That I start to wonder
Are you even larger
Are you that unknown
May be, may be not

When I visit Sunderbans and Nilgiris
or see pictures of astonishing Amazon
and read the science of the species
The eco system that exists so seamlessly

and yet much remains to be known
That I wish to know
If you are there too
Are you that unknown
May be, may be not

When I travel in the Arabian desert
and run after the sand and the mirage
understanding its diversity
of the biologically rich habitats
and yet much remains to be known
That I become inquisitive
Are you beyond that horizon
Are you that unknown
May be, may be not

When I visit the place of worship
irrespective of diversity in rituals
with a common intent and faith
I start to look within
and try to dig into the soul
to remove the ignorance
and yet much remains to be known
That I begin to believe
Are you there too
Are you that unknown Sakshi
May be, may be not